*Lares / Manes*

*Also by Billy Mills*

Genesis and Home
Triple Helix
Letters from Barcelona
Five Easy Pieces
The Properties of Stone
Tiny Pieces
A Small Book of Songs
What is a Mountain?
Logical Fallacies

# Billy Mills

# Lares / Manes
## Collected Poems

Shearsman Books
Exeter

Published in the United Kingdom in 2009 by
Shearsman Books Ltd
58 Velwell Road
Exeter EX4 4LD

www.shearsman.com

ISBN 978-1-84861-046-0
First Edition

Copyright © Billy Mills, 2009.

The right of Billy Mills to be identified as the author of this work
has been asserted by him in accordance with the Copyrights,
Designs and Patents Act of 1988.
All rights reserved.

### Acknowledgements

*Genesis and Home, Triple Helix, What is a Mountain?* and *Logical Fallacies* were all first published by hardPressed Poetry. *Properties of Stone* was first published by Bob Cobbing's Writers' Forum. *A Small Book of Songs* was first published by Wild Honey Press. *Five Easy Pieces* was first published by Shearsman Books. My thanks to all the publishers and to the editors of the many magazines and small pamphlets who also published parts of these works.

Some of the previously uncollected work has appeared in *Free Verse, Default, . . . in blossoms atop reeds it flares, Origin Series 6*, as a Kore broadsheet and as a pamphlet from Longhouse Press. Again, my thanks to all concerned.

Cover photograph copyright © Catherine Walsh, 2009.

## Contents

| | |
|---|---|
| Genesis and Home | 9 |
| Triple Helix | 35 |
| Letters from Barcelona | 67 |
| Five Easy Pieces | 93 |
| Properties of Stone | 117 |
| A Small Book of Songs | 161 |
| What is a Mountain? | 215 |
| Logical Fallacies | 279 |
| *Previously Uncollected Work* | |
|     A Small Book of Birds | 299 |
|     Paper Places | 307 |
|     Two Rivers | 330 |

In memory of my mother, Dee Mills, 1932–2008

GENESIS AND HOME
(1979–1985)

"... thou didst not enquire their meaning nor their cause. Hadst thou done so, the King would have been restored to his health and his dominion in peace. Whereas from henceforth he will have to endure battles and conflicts and his knights will perish, and wives will be widowed, and maidens will be left portionless, and all this because of thee."

from the *Peredur Ap Evrawc*

## *Genesis One*

1. it is no easy task to measure the distance
   in twin parts which were to procreate,
   the two effects compensate exactly

2. the egg of the world:
   sowing by night and cultivating by day,
   before gestation was complete

3. the building of the second sanctuary:
   a little shaky when you get up towards
   the speed of light

4. that the universe is uniform
   is a sign of the coming of water

5. who measured the spectra of galaxies;
   who was androgynous

6. the argument is mildly mathematical,
   our universe is so transparent

7. imagine a large cube of rubber,
   a universe in motion

8. "a dark cold place full of bright objects"

9. local knowledge of the past

## Follow the Makers' Instructions

1.     open
         carefully
   (the well oiled surface
   facilitating entry)

   avoid
   stretching and straining,
   unnecessary damage.

   this, you may find,
   prolongs the sensation

2.     unroll a little
   leave empty spaces

   it doesn't have to be
   an interruption

   the handlers identity
   is unimportant

3.     do not scratch!

       this
   guarantees protection

4.     beware
         of parthenogenesis

   use only once;
   a single seed
   can cause fertility

## *Genesis Two*

1. their great riches for offerings:
   the mountains and the seas

2, for the performance of rites:
   the uncertainty in the observational determination

3. distance is roughly linear
   observed in visible light

4. physically conceivable structures—
   the reed and forest for the work of building

5. a variation of more than a hundred
   regular patches of light

6. a certain magic density

three hens around the door
a cast iron stove
that never really works
quite as it should
a tilly hissing light into the room

the near successful crops
of aubergines and maize
pulses and grains
bought eighty miles away
a compost heap
the unused hands on tools
inchoate web of feelings
               summoned up
by field tree mist and stream:
cos in a patchwork frame

## Genesis Three

1. the spectrum of sunlight,
   before the beginning of the earth

2. in an evolving universe

3. the mountain had been shaped,
   to the sea its limit—
   the great distances implied

4. we look in their direction and it is dark

*Garlic*

because
of its virtue /
this pungency's
your perfume

a poor mans treacle
      its oil
is sulphurous / volatile
    but delicate
when gently simmered

I crush a clove
  into what soon will be
today's shared meal

## *Genesis Four*

1. details of the process were quite unknown,
    a natural consequence of the high temperatures

2. in slightly different form;
    variable light is unknown,
    subject to laws

3. has power over all things,
    composed as a sure foundation

4. candidates for association
    in a rich soil

5. "often in error, never in doubt"

## *To Make Elderberry Wine*

in September gather
the bunches of purplish-
black berries

strip from the stalks
with a fork
(this will stain
your fingers)

crush and add boiling
water (a gallon
to 3 pounds of fruit)
cool

and add yeast:
after 3 days strain
onto sugar

ferment in a dark jar

## *Genesis Five*

1. observation is of vital importance
   with the same intensity in all directions

2. the epoch of high density
   as an embryo, giving birth to fire

3. as they conceived
      insight applies
   to localised phenomena

4. whose shadow is immortality:
   incompatible with existing ideas

5. the sun is given a firm support
   measured out within the atmosphere

6. processes depend sensitively
   on the temperature assumed

## *Plague Years (after Boccaccio)*

some held a sober and
abstemious life
        reduced the risk
and lived in isolation

withdrawn to peaceful comfort
they passed the time
                    consuming modestly
the finest meat add drink
music and other sport
avoiding news and contact with
the outside world

others maintained the opposite
allowing no better medicine than
to drink
        be merry
whatever they desired
treating the whole thing as
      a wondrous joke
they held their homes
as common property
and all might come and go
just as they pleased

being careful, also, to avoid
the dying

## *Genesis Six*

1. this mountain flows
     a source
   from the roots of plants

2. out of this illuminating pattern
   came pure light and built the sky

3. the distribution of these sources over the sky
          which cannot be revised
   in their intrinsic brightness

4. will the night sky remain dark?

5. the arrow of time
   equivalent of blood

## *Plague Years (Protect and Survive)*

here is a checklist / between two huge fires /
stay at home / no poultry should be eaten / build
an inner refuge

have you chosen? / the poisonous atoms fly about
/ DO NOT GO OUTSIDE / essence consisting of rue /
stay at home / place the body in another room

evaporate on glowing bricks / between two huge
fires / listen for instructions / the poisonous
atoms fly about / deadly dangerous / no poultry
should be eaten

keep this booklet handy / read with care / keep
hands as clean as possible / here is a checklist
/ more dangerous at night

beyond that there can be severe damage / ye vain
supports / place the body in another room / DO NOT
GO OUTSIDE / essence consisting of rue / an air
attack is expected

## Genesis Seven

1. in the beginning there was nothing but water,
   highly unsuitable for the foundation

2. a lens shaped region of space,
   a chaotic mass like an egg

3. stir the water with an iron rod

4. almost no progress has been made

## *Plague Years*  *(Einstein 6/8/45)*

my universe is
the curves simplicity
conception of the mind
perfection non-visible
where all is energy
whose harmonies reveal
in what occurs
beyond the limits of
the merely we

others have forced this form
these flowering numerals
into their action at
a distance world
anthropocentrically
the mass of their inertia
has bent these figures
to their will

                and here
where the impossibly
parallel lines meet
they forge destruction
from this entelechy

tensor and root
        my formulae
cannot contain this deed

## *Genesis Eight*

1. some to the mountains, some to the desert,
   some to the plains,
   there appears to be no way out

2. the mysteries of the initial creation
   scattered the seeds before them

3. the local conditions need not be excessive:
   no light, nothing but darkness

4. the powers of objects and natural forces:
   red ochre, white clay, white stone

5. the veins were of turquoise;
   unable to remain in equilibrium

6. its attractive power likewise increases,
   which leads to some surprising and weird effects

## *Glendalough Forest Walk*

1. this is a glacial valley
2. a dying oak
3. this pool, a fine example of erosion
4. notice the peculiar growth involved
   in adapting to changing circumstances
5. roots are exposed by wear
6. the erotic may, the birch
   growing at an unnatural angle
7. holly / rowan / oak
8. the oak-victim of empire and industry
9. the cycle of life and death
10. here you can see the trees grow
    if you wait 50 years
11. oregon pines, imported for telegraph poles
12. rock lies under everything
13. the squirrel, Ratatoskr, sower of discord
14. or living in harmony
    a plant community
15. these trees are seen as nothing more
    than units in the overall economy
16. regeneration
    a young oak springs from a dead stump
17. only the oak's grotesqueness
    saves it from the axe
18. the end of the trail

## *Genesis Nine*

1. they started at sunrise, and were back by sunset;
   distant matter influences local events

2. the universe is observed not to rotate
   until the world is made over

3. other matter in the universe
   loosely speaking, from infinity

4. to be numerically reasonable,
   no sun, no moon, no stars

the seed "swells
    but this
must not be taken
as a sign of growth"

the elements required
are water, light,
hydrogen, time,
    (compress
a vast cloud
of gas and dust
      until
gravity takes over)
energy and earth.

## Genesis Ten

1. its origin, its structure, and its ultimate fate

2. everything was resting in perpetual darkness, more violent and active at these early epochs

3. search patiently amongst the tall white grass under extreme conditions of density

4. this process is repeated for many days and nights

5. no obvious trend or correlation is manifest but the end cannot be delayed overlong

......... rosemary  
the herb of memory  
friendship  
        fidelity  
thrives in a light dry soil  

I found some growing  
      near the wall  
in full flower  
delicate blue against  
the dark green leaf

## *Genesis Eleven*

1. flowing inside the crystal lattice
   it dwelt with the feeble glimmering,

2. and produced the atmosphere which is above us
   to pervade the whole of each entity

3. from the nothing the abundance
   in an even more violent state

4. from the conception the increase,
   an inescapable motion to the centre

5. to behave in unexpected ways

you make some salad,
peel and slice
onion, grate
carrot, shred
some cabbage,

slice mushrooms
thinly, cut
green and red
peppers, it's
reassuring to watch

## *Genesis Twelve*

1. the night shrinks from the ineffective
   multiplying in the passing time

2. lack of certainty in all things
   at the time when the earth became hot

3. can energy have a purpose?

4. that chaos must always increase,
   the night gave birth

5. the questions themselves are somehow invalid,
   the land disappears into them

6. the behaviour of matter under extreme conditions
   overshadowed the stream
                         overshadowed the mountains

7. their automatic character is becoming clear

# Triple Helix
(1984–86)

## Eleven Steps or Stages

        the countryside
is a place to visit
with the right equipment

cameras     a book
on wild flowers
on mushrooms

a field guide
to ancient monuments

a good pair of boots

this should provide
sufficient protection

*Leonardo: A Sketch*

observe & analyse
the waters swirl
plaited hair

eddy & spume
the warp
of muscle: bone

frozen in light
androgyne
vigour & dream

a face disfigured by
no halfwit
gioconda dream

what love survives
is in the ordinary

not
moments of ecstasy

corn
no not corn
run on ahead

& wonder
could it be
barley

in the first instance
particles spin:
illusion of substance

touch the surface:
probable spin
entirely undetected

sap rises
& the leaf unfurls

most important
most neglected

a sensor
of impulse

converted
to sound

\*

the point of contact
reproduction begins

begins to wear
from the first use

\*

ensure that the weight is adjusted

\*

clean
upgrade
replace

a proper motion
stars recede
imperceptibly

but the seedbeds
are local phenomena
energy & earth

from this
extrapolate
backwards

the squirrel climbed
with a message
from the snake
to the eagle

& the squirrel said:

they left shadows
for memorial

that day

it's easy to see
that this is not a picture:
no frame, no focus

stop
would you me like to tell you
what you see?

stop

        the valley
        stretches out below
        a small flock of goats
        & something in the water
        that does not belong

retelling this story
as if it were my own

# Clusters / A Map

## *Found Objects*

about two miles
from the house
where my parents now live:
the crannog of Lagore

'the first great lacustrine retreat
noticed in Ireland
in modern times'

was found in 1840
by workers
digging drains

a raised circular mound
about 520 feet across

200 tons of bones
removed for manure

once
on a visit
I walked over

& could see
from the road
the yellow bog

but found no path
& was reluctant
to climb the wall
& look for gaps

in hedges
& so went back to the village
for a pint

(reading about Lagore in Wood-Martin's book, I can't help but
be amazed by his confident Victorian belief that one could cram
everything there is to know about something into one big book
and close the covers)

go to Kildare St.
to the National Museum
and you can see:

an iron grisset (for melting tallow)
bronze keys
four knives
a fishing spike
a flint arrowhead
a sickle a bill-hook
a spade head
a baked clay tuyere
a bronze omega brooch
a prisoner's collar & chain

an enigma:
this semi-derelict shop

window panes
on the roof

a sign peeling
but readable

**THE DUNGEON**

funny
to find it so interesting

yet make
no enquiries

across the car park
the white outline of a man
stark on a black wall

*Thousands of objects dating from the 11$^{th}$– 13$^{th}$ centuries have been found at the site of the Dublin Civic Offices site on Wood Quay. They include pottery, personal objects in bronze, various wooden and iron items and coins.*

*In addition the remains of structures—including timber houses and fences—were found, along with two planks containing sketches of Viking-type ships.*

(The Irish Times 04/12/1973)

   the rock
is mainly glacial drift
with raised beach
   at the eastern end

between the bluffs
 of glacial till
the river
   & the pool
beneath a low hill
on the southern side

*longphort*
ship-fort
winter quarters

& they built
house over house
a new one
every twenty years

and ate
cattle and pigs
some sheep
horseflesh and fish

a porridge
made from seeds
of goosefoot and knotgrass
onion and grain

(and built a kingdom)

*Henry II, King of England, Duke of Normandy and Aquitane, notifies that he has granted and confirmed to his men of Bristol his city of Dublin, to be inhabited and held by them from him and his heirs, with all liberties and free customs which they have at Bristol and throughout his entire land.*

Dublin 1171/2

and the people:

*More severe punishment than hitherto to be inflicted on regraters, who purchase flesh and other victuals coming to the city and sell them in small parcels privately, thus greatly raising prices on the people.*

if the city is home
      is *domus*
& must be integral

then what are we to make
of our antipathy

who have to share
this home?

the buddleia
    (a Chinese import)
is everywhere

rooting between
the bricks
of crumbling walls

or rampant
in shallow soil
on vacant spaces

elder & alder are common
yarrow for divination

## *Hexagram*

Triangulation: a series of points whose
absolute and relative positions are known.

A particle which helps constitute a
person at one instant may be at the centre
of a star at the next. This is not an
exaggeration.

Interpretation: not metaphor, not allegory,
not fable.

Lichens are, generally, a composite of a
fungus and an alga, in a symbiotic state.
The new whole is quite distinct from
either of the two constituents.

When instructed on the screen, key in
your personal number on the keyboard.
If the number is incorrectly keyed, the
machine will invite you to key in your
number again. The machine will allow
you make three attempts after which it
will  retain your card.

Finally, if you cannot manage to get
yourself unstuck by any of the above
methods, then you will have to wait for
help to come.

## The Map

At this point, I had thought to tell a story, but I think I'll show you this letter instead:

**NEW RATHMINES CONSTITUENCY**

As you know the boundaries for Dublin Corporation constituencies have been changed. I thought you might like to see the outline of your new area which is called "Rathmines Constituency" and I attach a map which shows this with some detail. If you have any queries about this or any other matters arising in your constituency please feel free to contact me.

This is an election year
and the map is so small
and so badly photocopied
as to be virtually useless.

## *At Vermeer's Window*

take three rooms
       a few friends
the ordinary days

this quiet house
       in a familiar city
a muted conversation

or music
       or a letter
read, a letter answered

it is, perhaps,
       sufficient to describe
this colder, northern light

## TRANSPOSED CONFIGURATIONS

A native of China, it was introduced into these islands in the late 17$^{th}$ century by an Irish forester, Augustine Henry, and became a popular garden shrub. Although almost unknown in the wild in Dublin only 20 years ago, it has become perhaps the most commonly found weed in the city.

## LIFE AS      LAND

is no insurance

it is
         instead
a sign
of accidence

as tangents
         define
circle

significant
omission

         build
erasure

uncertain
destinations

The question he should have asked, when he got there, when he found the place, when he saw it. The question that would have opened the door.

"Who do you work for?"

Which addresses itself.
Which addresses the question.
Which addresses itself correctly.

Is this sufficiently coherent?

in a dynamic universe
stillness is difficult

The people who live in Peter Pan's Palace
refuse to accept their responsibilities.
        Is this why they are immobile?
        Is this why they live in two dimensions?

I could
        at this stage
make a map

but who needs a map
        when you don't
know
where you are

or where
you want to go

With these varieties, as I understand it, the plants will flower and seed in the normal way, but the seeds will not be fertile. The only way to produce a second generation is to repeat the entire process of hybridisation. Every time.

In what direction are we headed?

To what extent can, or should, the direction be imposed?


& than night
I slept there
& had a dream

& in that dream
nothing happened

# Letters from Barcelona

(1987–88)

*One*

so much culture amongst
the dirt—the air
laden—the city selling
itself on hoard-

ings designed by Miró
to shoppers in el corte
inglés or the de-
formed limbs exposed

on the metro "tengo
hambre" the sign
says I have hunger
walking the streets in

the Barrio Gótico
the bread is sub-
stantiated air—ring-
ing with "butano

butano" where note
follows note in un-
expected un-
suspected order as

Santa Lucia—
clean lines after
grandiloquent saints next
door—the smell of the

sewer the smell of
the sea reminding
the desiccate river
"are only for

those who can write
a faultless fugue straight
away with no need to
correct it" attending

the dry disks of
honesty (Lunaria
biennis) in memory
as the wind an-

swers "not conspicuously"
the strings plangency
in a certain garden
held as

instigator—the plane
of a tear on the plane
of a cheek in
the widows palace—

fingers and bow on
the strings the narrow
streets turning back
to the no longer ri-

ver the birds and flowers
their vendors in cantus
firmus— the burden
of air attend-

ed in a kind of
attenuated exile
ordering perceptions
(how many?

and their names?) we sit
on the fifth floor and
listen to pigeons
on the roof "with con-

venient notes" the litter
lays down a map
of the city as used
regathering daily

in an order of tones
the streets turn back on
themselves as we listen
to the cello

sustaining the note
while playing gains firmness
with confidence
sustaining the move-

ment into another
quarter—attending
again the firm song
borrowed the val-

ue implied in walking
to come at last to
no conclusion no
resolution

*Two: Notes and Postcards*

 in the rational
          city
 a grid laid down

 (ideal for walking)

*The extreme example of the predator-swamping tactic is probably represented by the periodic cicadas, which possess one of the most extraordinary life histories of any insect.*

the idea
      an ideal
of order

runs down
      (the garden)
to the river

(terraced)
      a mirror
not a mirror

as here
      green
on gray

a balcony
      & pigeons
from roof

to roof
      wing-tips:
clapping

*Once a pool of semi-stagnant,
slow-moving water has been formed,
several forces maintain the status
quo.*

    wind
        in the tunnel
    a train draws near

*As in the mayflies, synchronized emergence may enable an individual to increase its chance of avoiding predatory attack simply because there are too many victims for the predators in the area to consume . . . despite the fact that cicadas evidently are attractive prey for many animals.*

eyes
      like cats
our neighbours
      feed

flowers
      on
balconies
      show

people
      who made
the effort
      "my wife's

music
      saves me
a lot
of words"

the Call*
      quiet
Sunday
      turning

on questions
      of value
or measure
      a new

tonality
      the meaning
hidden
      an island

of voices
    still
Bach on
    the radio

tocar
    to feel
to play
    an

instrument
    to chime
to touch
    on others

a succession
of cities:

        the cleanest
quietest streets
are underground
(& oldest)

plaques
in the graveyard

what's left of
houses

jars
for oil and grain



*what makes peatland different*
*from other habitats is simply*
*that it is unbalanced*

*(La Terrasse: after Braque)*

| | | |
|---|---|---|
| the | wood-grain a splash of | yellow |
| yellow | colour  the warped table | the |
| echoes | a jug glass and spoon | echoes |
| the | | white |
| white | | the |
| the | | white |
| white | the furniture was here yesterday and was | the |
| echoes | different and it will be here tomorrow a | echoes |
| the | nd it will be different and you and I wo | yellow |
| yellow | n't notice but the painter notices again | the |

*a narrow way
an alley
the Jewish quarter

                    "turning
          others leaves"

          or tending
          to obfuscate:

          to walk
                    (unexpectedly)
          into the scent

          of broom

the casual
    everyday
violence:

the bus-queue
not the knives

in the Barrio Chino



*. . . having adapted to an
environment where the only
supply of mineral nutrients
comes from rainfall.*

## *A Song*
**(from the Spanish)**

single
and alone
with no family

married
four children
and no job

pregnant
and sleeping
in the streets

charity
I don't want
I want to work

help me:
*un duro*
*por favor*

(we understood
nothing) an actual

cello in an actual
bookshop: a student

cold-starting the suite
the streets contriving

to bring us
nowhere: precisely

that speech is most like
music uncomprehended

*Presumably the noise produced by hundreds or thousands of chorusing cicadas also has a deterrent effect on some of the cicada's enemies.*

planning the poem
planning the trip
(by bus) to the mountains

to places drained
(for us) of one
significance

to be invested with
another    where every
step involves

an agitation of
insects  that such
buildings (*Taull*) sprang

from such villages
as symbols attesting
the limpidity of stone

of air thin in
the august heat
unmoving remembered

in displacement:
the ornate sardana
turns to the sound

of brass (as the city
turns) to the sound
of a culture

in search of itself
and finding?
song in the metro

a child's hand
extended     the voice
insistent

christopher
columbus

uncovered
america

it's possible?

*Three*

six pot-plants on
the balcony are
Barcelona in flower
fixed by (to our

minds) inadequate
metal hoops
the city puts on
beauty to municipal

orders and we buy it
we buy the flowers
the hoops machines
for the kitchen the

streets are transposed
by fireworks observing
the changes involved
in learning the air

humid the idea
of colour of birds
returning where stone
records water

in Sant Felip Neri
"a description of
a state of language
at a given

moment" the music
is stilled but
the voices continue
the dancers inventing

tradition (Sunday)
in Plaça Sant Jaume
the city as
museum or the

unswept streets these
"almost sunless alleys"
where cats meet
to gather the elements

of music a science
of the city exposing
the roots
remembering stones

in Empuries
the too-loud radio
next door "in order
to place the birth

of the Colonia
Barcino" the
rhythm and pitch
of pigeons in streets "laid

down by the romans"
this (articulate) almost
silence after
the signs written

on cardboard requiring
assistance: to think
in a different
language in lieu

of a garden "an
interesting street"
cheap music and
the poverty disguised

as aggression
"necesito una
ayuda" the sign
says "posat guapa"

as the fireworks
re-echo the city
responding the flowers
prosper or die

enquiring we
walk the streets
to come again to this
after the bin-men after

the day defined
by speech by voices
and cars in the street
the sizzle and smell of

meat from the lower
flats these intensify
proximate others
our unknown neighbours

**FIVE EASY PIECES**
(1982–1991)

*Reading Lorine Niedecker*

who told her second husband
      (after they married)
"I am a poet"

    'a what?"

      ★

the silence
    singing

      ★

    the poem
    (let us confess it)
    is not immutable

    nor is the river

      ★

   of flesh
      (carnelian)
   bones of white quartz

      ★

there is a river
in this city

          sluggish
          mud-grey
          not given to flooding

          carrying too much history

    \*

          wintergreen (pipsissewa)
          astringent, tonic, alterative

\*

and Darwin wrote:

    "I have been making
some little trifling observations
which have interested
    and perplexed me
much."

## "the stony field"

    the slow accretion
    of detail

        things made over
    reused, renewed
    so that nothing is wasted

    thus we will sometimes
    say:

        lets cook
    some extra potatoes

    and fry them
        in the morning
    for breakfast

*As I was led to keep in my study during many months worms in pots filled with earth, I became interested in them, and wished to learn how far they acted consciously, and how much mental power they displayed.*

a small rosette of leaves
pulled in

to block
    or guard
the entrance

"a curious little book"

"has been received
with almost
laughable enthusiasm"


about 400 copies remain, stored in the top of my wardrobe, as a reminder of the quantity of error, the error of quantity


*I was thus led to conclude that all the vegetable mould over the whole country had passed many times through, and will again pass many times through, the intestinal canals of worms*



        that this work
        done from

        a private
        necessity

        should benefit
        the totality



this detail
discovered by accident:

      an old man
          bent
      in his garden

      to measure
      the gradient

      & degree
      of movement

      of earth
      extruded


. . . the field was always called by my sons 'the stony field'. When they ran down the slope the stones clattered together. I remember doubting whether I should live to see these larger flints covered with vegetable mould and turf. But the smaller stones disappeared before many years had elapsed, as did every one of the larger ones after a time; so that after thirty years . . . a horse could gallop over the compact turf from one end of the field to the other, and not strike a single stone with his shoes.




    strangely
(or not so strangely)
I've begun to notice them everywhere

little, vermicular structures
      of earth
and intestinal juices

        still active
this mild
        December
though normally
they burrow

to some depth
and form a chamber
where
        "one

or several worms
will pass the winter
        rolled up
into a ball"

tonight
the moon is silent

that is
invisible

but the room
is illuminated

by an occasional
           passing
                      car

## *A Small Love Song*

eyes
and the lips
and the hands
and the form
of a woman
coming through the door

signifying nothing
    but a woman
coming through the door

*it helpeth such as are bursten
and that have broken the bone of the legge*

hear
you are here

and this
is what it's like:

hello
come in
sit down
you're welcome

absorb the menstrual flow / there is
no odour / gentle, flexible and sensitive guide

now you are ready / following the
natural curve / the knotted cord remains

the angle of insertion / made from
natural materials / it is important to
relax / there is strong resistance

a touch or
the smell
of your smell
as I remember it

but carefully

for love
is not denied

by chance
or circumstance

a single
dandelion

on a heap
of rubble

defiantly
    (for the moment)
golden

## Finding the Comfrey

below the house
across the field
in a corner
by the stream
where the tractor cannot reach

the largest blackberries I have ever seen

in the ditches
at the lower ends of the fields

the sign
is not the thing

the sign
is an indefinite article

the sign on the rock
in the field
beside our landlord's house

the sign said

*FOR GOD AND ULSTER*


in this
precise
place

at this
precise
time

precisely

*Anyone who is unable to determine the direction of the Qibla must ask someone who knows. If there is no one to ask, then one decides what one thinks to be the right direction and performs the prayer in that direction. If one discovers he was praying in the wrong direction, one's prayer will still be correct and no repetition is required. Should one know the right direction while the prayer is in progress, he should turn to that direction without interrupting one's prayer.*

after the third
cut
of silage


a curlew looks
for her missing home




that a sense of community is not the same thing as a bunch of
more-or-less like-minded people getting on each other's nerves



I am relearning
the names of the weeds

that house again

the one with the tilly and the hens

funny that a few unsuccessful months in a place can come to seem so important

in retrospect

sharing despite
our mutual
incomprehension

the maculate
imperfect
stillness

of just such a day

and finding the comfrey

*Departures*

the short slope
a carpet
of yellow caps

& me
picking
& smiling

these
will dry
nicely

The night of the lunar eclipse; some
lunatic driving his car on the frozen
lake, practising handbrake turns.


*(after Sappho)*

moon is down
& the seven sisters

past midnight;
the city sleeps

I am alone


in a city without gardens;
the Eurosex Snack Bar

in a city without gardens;
the park is the place to be

in a city without gardens;
voices next door: fighting

       this bears down
       this lays bare
       this drives
       this shatters & destroys


thin fleshed, hygrophagous, slimy or
sticky, dark olive grey-brown or yellow
-brown when moist, in dry conditions
leathery yellow, smooth glabrous, with
greeny spots


      *(for Larry)*

      a poem
      is always a poem

      a moth
      a moth

      even
      a stranger

      caught
      in a room

      finding
      no exit

in a park
by a river
in another city

not the one I was born in
not the one I live in now

a city at war
with itself




a map
a grid
a model

the art
of the fugue
on the stereo

PROPERTIES OF STONE

*Neither is there a smallest part of what is small, but there is always a smaller (for it is impossible that what is should cease to be). Likewise there is always something larger than what is large. And it is equal in respect of number to what is small, each thing, in relation to itself, being both large and small.*

Anaxagoras; Fr. 3
(from Kirk & Raven: *The Presocratic Philosophers*)

# Lapidary

## *Aragonite*

orthorhombic

white, grey,
green or
violet

vitreous

transparent to
translucent

'yt is gud
 and lyght to bere'

expanding

such forms
are imaginable

(this little book)

as the surface
of a sphere

occurs
in the shells
of certain animals

(corals & clams)

'I do not suppose
the truth of all

or so much as
the tenth part

of these

wonderful properties'

volume
proportional to pressure
in inverse

if temperature
is constant

& in deposits
around hot springs

## *Basalt*

running
to catch
the giants

    (she ran
     we followed)

prisms
of stone

steps
to the sea

& village
(emporion)

walled
a system

of pipes
& filters

admitting
desire

to communicate
relations

judge
(from the landscape)

the rock
beneath

## *Carnelian*

sol y luna
the dancing giants
of La Merc,

pipes & drums

'recreates the minde
cohibits sad dreams
expels fear'

the silicates:
reddish or brownish types
called sard or carnelian

    cooling
    & clumping
    to form galaxies

light: the dominant
    constituent

matter: a negligible
    contamination

the giants    run
stop
        twirl
stop

   : aiding
    or guiding
    in discovery

ragnarok
(correfoc)
this stone

stanches blood
& restrains anger

*

'I have made
yis lytill buke . . .
for my selfe

and for a few
of my frendes'

## *Emerald*

lulled by the murmuring vowels
*te quiero verde*
the tired old phrases

but music inheres
in the clash of ideas:

patterns of light
      traced
in the evening air
as strategy

this stone gives eloquence
foreshadowing

the male signals
the female
      selects

transfusing the air
with green
over meadow      marsh

the cyclosilicates:
(this song
is pseudo-referential)

patterns of colour
duration
intensity

or chooses to respond
announcing position

the presence
of chromium
which soothes the eyes

restores what was lost
& strengthens memory

males who respond
to false signals

are captured
   & eaten

## Flint

*(for Catherine)*

an opaque dull-coloured amorphous
silicate rock the stream of matter
slowed by the stream of light walking
(in July rain) the walls of Canter-
bury *tô tí?* 'No simpler mechanism
would enable it to do as well what
its users expect.' occurs as nodules
in chalk cooling & trapping the neutral
atom in optical molasses momentum
(to sing of love) transferred as an
exchange of particles whose walls are
fields of force containing
emotion

## *Figures in a Landscape (Granite)*

she is turning
& saying                    masses of rock

something
& he

is listening                a jumble
                            of tiny
grass                       crystals
is growing

rocks
scattered                   feldspar
                            & quartz

a sparrow

& flowers:
stamen & pistil

frozen                      flecks
                            of mica
the spine
curved                      a formless
                            tangle
to hear
meaningless                 can be smoothed
words                       & polished

## *Jasper*

reddish
chert-like
of fine crystals

this stone
frightens phantoms

as measure
of energy
conferring

speed
of thought
& action

(to realize
that where you are
is not the place

& turn
& head off

not knowing
where you're going)

systems
in uniform
motion

the arc
of a stone

dropped
from a train

in the sphere
of Thrones

(a poetic?)

(& venomous beasts)

## *Limestone*

the system
an act therein:

'. . . pick up a piece
of common limestone.

There are probably
    fossils
in it.'

calcite & dolomite
who would speak of love
speaks of 3 types

| | | |
|---|---|---|
| organic | → | from the skeletons of living things |
| chemical | → | evaporite sequence |
| | → | oolites |
| detrial | → | allochthonous |

these rules
(or observations)
are purely descriptive

      ★ ★ ★

over grey stones
    streams of heat
un(     )
    (    )

until ringlake
         had(          )
(                )
         where the baths were
then in(          )
         (            )
(          )
     that is royal thing
how the(     )
     (     )city(     )

             *


of a body
of language

## *Marble*

the problem is: we read
& write for reasons as
the stone recrystallizes
in heat a list of street
names in a story lines
in a grid of places the
intrusion of igneous
matter descriptions
of two friends of marble
is white when pure
some stuff about critical
density / eternal recurrence

⋆

to have come this far
& to have seen these things
& to have failed to ask why

*Obsidian*

the small waves break
yards from the tracks
in corrugated moonlight

the small notes interweave

black bottle-glass
(this stone was used
for weapons)

        our train
        is late again

in the complete absence
of crystals
the double helix reads

in both directions

        (cellular
        grammar)

the moonlight the
sea the waiting
are held

in the music of
bats round the station
lights on the hill

## Quartz

over the river
the great tomb gleaming
in a pattern of reuse          repopulation

/

'to make a shyning water'

/

these fragments of coloured stone
laid out to form a picture
to walk on

/

white   pink   green
or the pure transparent

/

in crystals a flaw
allows growth

/

exposed to sun and salt air

/

the path to the hostel
above the bay

scattered stones
catching moonlight

## *Sapphire*

night &
rain

headlights
through

my parents'
window:

breath
on my shoulder

nothing
to say

## *Of Isostasy: Eastbourne*

the tongue against the
alveolar ridge is
the english tradition: birds
insects, flowers (their la-

tin) to lines from campion's
lyre not the slow grind of
stone but vowel music
the motion occurs

on lines an island di-
vided 'on mechanical
principles' a hap-
hazard pattern: failure

the stillness unstable
'the movements themselves are facts
of observation'
a language occluded

riding the stars the breath
over the pain combining
a set of symbols &
the motion of waves

a position comprising
complacency seen in
the absence of rhythm
or 'who do you serve?'

a series of rules
implying the waters
(a syntax) defined in a
system of dynamic

balance shingle reflects
an inexplicable
moon in the garden:
friday & shattered glass

gathering specimens
of isostasy: Eastbourne
by moonlight the artist
contrives these effects

in the absence of meaning
the small stars evade
our competence: feeling
the properties of stone

are silence & stillness
promoting the objects
rigidity tending
to stasis; language

a sequence of movements
& failures: to ask
the unexpected question
in chiaroscuro

the pier etched clearly
to seaward: coloured balls
of light defining the
principle: that motion's a

function of painting
the child: his furniture
or the study of history
in the absence of time

after the labour the stars
expounding a perfect
exhaustion ( these lines
inscribed in the margins)

a stream of articulate
movements    language
a question of service
unlocking the darkness

a story unfolding
in the absence of tone:
this umbrella hurled to mark
a beginning 'a

problem of pressure' or
sleep interrupted again
that arc a music
of sequences the cold

room or listening against
bells incipient
a work of synthesis
(Durham) colour of sun

then snow harpsichord & birds
yellow sandstone a peal
persistent to mark
a particular day

nocturne: a stillness after
delivery the street-
lights extinguished
assault on the sentence

in the absence of
evidence the yellow
croci seen from my classroom
window defining the

symbols the sign defining
the signified (a
system of relatives)
this darkness contriving

fecundity riding
the pain the woman breathing
(there are lines: connecting
stars through freezing air)

shingle & groynes
a concord of motion (my love
& I out walking)
articulate dance of

water through stones the result
not a cause of motion
the child (Durham) latent
in snow or later

a sharpness in the absence
of words the chalk shows
green into white the lines
spears into staves prick

to victorian prudery
a dozen foreigners
(me & my students)
descending on england

the role & status
of children: a pattern
of fragments the river
(invisible) imposes

a shape on the streets
these elders awaiting
armageddon in Eastbourne
a settlement     rhythm

& texture of moments
repeated 'the drinks
are in the kitchen' a push
then silence the taxi

after the bleeding
the fumbling towards system
or freedom describing
a temporary stillness

## *Landscapes*

**'I hate scenery'**

settlement & flux: a
discrete series
of occasions moving
to an approximate rhythm
of domestic rituals

instance the door
in the hillside quartz
in the slant of
sunshine repeated evading
expected particulars

the irksome familiarity
of dereliction seen
in a cultural capital
squandered (The Dublin
Experience) comforting

certainties sustaining
an illusion of meaning
remembered a network
of echoes enabling
nothing

This is not unusual, for the present seldom respects the observer's sense of diffusion. Given the way in which this volume differs from other books on the subject of arrangement, differences which arise from its wider than usual range of interests, we should beware of using it in re-evaluating the standard accounts.

First the one, then some (imagined) other.

beyond
the factory

a grove
of olives

lizards
flit

steps
lead

another
lesson

sea
& trains

an iterated
series

days
stretches

& folds
rows

of vines
an order

of learning
forms

mountains
beyond

a stone the child picked remembers the sea
the white face eroded rests on the table
a clutter of things the stones run through
his fingers wet sand sticks discarded
bottles a spent condom we moved away from

are strange attractors the beach strewn with figures
developing strategies – a resolution
of tensions – harmony: the stones
rustle shells crunch walking the child explores

the land of the giants: movement &
stasis maintained a fresh alignment
to circle arms raised hands joined the steps
ordained bonds cement under pressure

the lush sea bed inadequate rainfall

for several years gulls nest opposite
or rest between flight & flight

      the child
points waves turns to another amusement
addresses the problem bringing the past
to bear

   the sea retains momentum
the mind its message moments of self-
similarity a picture of no-
thing the slow irredeemable progress
towards language (sufficient encoding)
to bear on the present

     concerning
a memory the child shares stones re-

luctantly shares the process of learning
naming the weather the ordinary
streets swing into focus to bear on
the future a series of postulates
the sea makes
                    the stones reorganize
in inevitable patterns

        stone
        slows

        streams
        cools

        layers
        form

        pillows
        beds

lights light flicker distant dimmer fog
on their channel other sounds the sea
saved cover your head sleep now see you
'night guard us dreaming silence a family
a new eruption

The two factors which most seem to distinguish the early scientific lapidaries from their magical predecessors are: (1) rationalization, and (2) the disclaimer.

Artíes: she
squats to piss
in a field of flowers

somewhere below
in another field
a farmer farms

a system of arbitrary symbols expressing
intention: innumerable discrete impacts
of stone on stone the tide rakes shingle
under the bandstand (november) invigorating
displacement of function pervades the repossessed
seafront salt air families take each other's
measure expecting the turn away from
the sea the wish tower the downs beyond

the strings unravel: waves
cross knowing photons
in a pattern
of probability

the light
circles
the head of a pin
(a transformation)

green fields seen
from a train
occasional

splashes of yellow
implying fecundity
the slow

monotonous roll
of particular
matter

detrial layers
laid under
the pressure

of time
the child
sleeps

heedless
of months spent
trying

to remember
*drumlin*

crossing the river
the smooth stones crossing
the valley & up
where air enabled
the driver's extravagant
laughter to stone
as artefact

completing the mountain
mycelium (Taüll)
spaced steps climbing
the spire in-
terior cool
the unfinished
road

clouds low on the downs
rain imminent (words)
gulls on the carpark
wheel the sea beyond

the centre
    hidden
an opening

folded: burst &
pause

    learning
conversation
the giants
    cogitate
the bisyllabic
question reaching
a temporary settlement

books beds the toys
scattered snatches
of silence rescued

the great wave
of stone exposed
on impact love

a kind of erosion:
telling stories
in imaginary
time

a child playing with bricks & sounds
discovers an order of colours: parents
the child raises a vaguely accusative finger
demanding the names of the elements
in memory the small walled fields run
to the cliff's edge the child builds
to destroy in a pattern of learning
a syntax misplaced toys words in the margin
the great wall's curve carved in the air
for protection . . .

a rhythm
of interaction

a question
of ownership
property
values
a landscape
of boundaries
a word
placed
so
on the page
the feather's
furl
making
the weather
a cat
crossing
the top
of the world
dodging
traffic
under
the gothic
a word
exchanged
on the metal
bridge:
making
the difference

listen a
song bird's
song train
beyond

car park
voices
child squeaks
talks

a radio
listen
the wind
child calls

morning
bird's gone
a bell

child's song

A Small Book of Songs

## Alba: In the Park

now is night come quietly
come to the park:

the ambiguous attraction of sweet simplicity
birds nest under the fascia derelict
inhabited house next door
or sing in the green the composite city

night after stars distant traffic
straight road long night cars
pass pitch rises   peaks   descends
conflated memories a string
of disjointed idioms cooling & slowing

energy condenses increasing complexity
receding light seen shift the background
measurable

       fionn uisce
       phoenix

       a column
       as pretext

a monument to mutual incomprehension
wings spread bird rises hollow music
intersect the great figure recumbent
grass damp (be near   where?) here

we are rayah (out there   where?) there
out over the sea the mountains
a token (ubiquitous) power measures
enter the light lamp lit decentre

difficult locked into others' preoccupations
a country enacting the long inevitable slide
into mediocrity altered a set
of suspended expectations

small square grey stone fountain
quiet sunday youth club museum
of footwear church front bullet marks

all the way up


        diggers
        & delvers
        mind

        a site
        experiment

        the park
        at night
        lights
        take on

        an emphasis
        distant
        colour

        the five
        directions
        an arc

        inscribed
        stick
        thrown

        the dog
        chased

over
the grass

not now
lines turn
tables
of incidence

(a theory)
hooks
        files
a network

storage
created
simplicities

follow
the content
learning
the song

'a field
of folk'

datable fragments dig down cut layers dust off outmoded notions
of beauty decay a section through memory inanimate
worlds persist 'a parody of plein air' morning is best
answer an answer of archaeology syntax offends
the specific question guessing at function slow rain descends
our son directs (inventively) the day's complexities
decay protects the uncertain evidence     moments of clarity
imagined in genuine gloom the river beyond the art
of reconstruction pattern the morning son up demanding
a continuous presence


day goes light fades over the car
park gathering greyness a weave of memories days spent
in the park playing at adult a fear of sentiment in
retrospect time communicates a problem with feeling
try to recapture places remembered warily night
clears slowly the mind of the sleeper clearing the radio
fumbling towards certainty fumbling the question evading
the day light ritual white dawn song

trying to get more in.

trying.
we walked. spoke. were
certain.

youthful. an exact-
ing science.
(lyric). accepting.

the burden.
of information. then.
innumerable.

bending the waves.
(trying). related.

the moments.

conversation. the long.
evenings. weaving.

sing.

write.

delete.

re-order.

landscape
an artefact.

trying.
to get.
more.
in.

who pays who decides
who passing the place
where memory remains

unfathomed speaks
the language of archetypes
mind of the asker

skin smooth under
fingers contours
the child stirs

clocks run back
-wards matter escapes
as energy: entropy

sites of emergence
waiting

moments of light
frozen the great
circle

(the proof
from photographs)

implied
patterns
of impact

a hierarchical structure. fragments. pictures. instances. whose daughters. selection. processing. retention. not yet fully understood. waiting. for a letter. answer.

to make (or find) an island.


meanders: the child
chases the sheep
chasing the river

chopper circles
cattle over
the water home

sites of emergence
the first devour
the later oh

nature nurture
genetic
imperatives

the repetition of experience day after
night in the park wander behind
childhood a set of images
in the shelters under

man with a bicycle ladder taper
gas wick on to the next one

flash: framing the mind

flash: ways in the balance/preys to
history

flash: deny the existence of questions?
conventions

under observe the child exploring
gravity deserted playground
wording precise

birds splash in the flooded gutter
wake to imaginary rain

## Ballad: Of Motion

one      two
me      you

walking the same way daily
insensate ritual delight
in motion    words signs
the centre escape me

mind invents structure
in fog on the downs
accents our isolation
ambiguous fallacies

outward & home
the small book of nature
explained these consequences
our difficult future

flying westward son
colouring rainbow fish
textural criticism
familiar fields random

mosaic descend again
rain echoes comparative
history of feeling    song
words echo mind's music

in canonical order
defining silence
a syntax suspended (verb)
the space between

one         two
me          you
breast      bone

start here notice
abnormal traces wind
leaves brittle memories
uncertain persuasion

waiting to move time
(conditionally) onwards
impossible voices question
connections stagnant sleep

a space (you have seen it)
ergative verbs
the same event
dispersed perspectives

knowing you don't know
road curves over
the bridge canal
& railway below

into the village
(a holiday) we have
come & are leaving
purchase

a family ticket
these silent mornings
comparison:
the art of memory

fire            home
      water

proportion is everything:
tower & square
rhyme an instinct
the ideal city

a single memory
internalized
streets necessary
the garden shimmers

step in the river
feel stability
& flux   words bend
under such pressure

night gathers line
forms this darkness
sit at the table
(genetic imperative)

naming the sound
time polyvalent
energy the core
vocabulary light

dims heat settles
presentation cephalic an-
terior we have been here
too long

```
one         two
me          you
breast      bone
fire        home
      water
```

### Canzo: Each To Its Mate

nothing is gathered

from nothing
              nothing comes

songs still
longing an
essence

thrush in
the garden
come

calmly
our children
sleeping

song stills
their breathing

memory: your hand
voice shadow
I wanted

something you had
but didn't know

skirting the central
isolate word
insidious follow

signs reluctant
desire's soft curve
radiant moistness

blush pink velvet
sinuous lines
(a fictive reality)

tones blend air
complex statements

bite the fruit
enter smooth strokes

soft now snatch
air out random
green emerging

now green now
everything not
love is sleeping

snatch the movement
random out
emerging moment

soft now snatch
random air
love not sleeping

slow                    slow

  each
    word
      works

here
this happened

love
unfolded

here
saw her
here spoke
here

hill
a park

trees

roads

dust

slow
the city
below

sea drags shingle dragging
the sea
      outwards & under
rustle & clink stone against
stone the value of silence
where language fails
love the question



      in his dream
      she loved him    waking
      the monitor sings
                  there blue
      here green    yellow
      the variegated hills

      light shifts clouds love
      the question

bird
through the window
look

autumn leaves

scattered traces

## Unfinished Alba

in his dream she loves him:
waking too

place names explained
remembered
       adumbrated
mapping the changes

stories (in this place
       this happened)
on indigo island

wind dominates

cobwebs lattice
iron frames

the bridge
    (an icon)
turgid

words wind shapes
trees our (rented)
doorway

       hills
illuminated

sun beyond rain

wind stirs the trees stirs
the storm's confusion
precipitate sounds
offer protection
our sleeping children

or call time softly
call fortuitous
silent affection
hair on the pillow
no longer perturbs

needs held long now
the vital question
limit the morning
serendipity
waking volition

movements remembered
insensate extend
phatic locutions
fondly this softness
our breathing fulfils

minor adjustments
the wind imposes
rain on the window
shaping affections
a form on the day

monitor static
alarm-clock song
distant traffic
asthmatic sawing

they came & they built & they organized
the landscape   solid dependable citizens
& this was the reason this explains nothing
you know the same few words writing themselves
repeatedly avoiding memorable phrases
light penetrates an imperfect record
torn membranes we share
                                            or reconstruct
these fragments   extract unwitting testimony
morning is morning parcels of energy
the space between our common consent
& closed eyes clearing dream & contingency
to begin again: not light nor music
but the word obliterate   defying silence

moonsilver fills the dark utility
grope for the nightfeed
apparently

           ordinary suburban
family child insistent
calls words inadequate
           (no pipes no
               sweet nymphs dancing)
contentment a rhythm
time
    turns

morning again waking resume
the pattern light distant voices
breath out winter silent cover
spill an insistent trace the park
in memory

waking this syntax bargain
love before language: stories
exact this essence call softly
calls sun between eye & cloud
a tone

iridescent this moment these hills
morning again taste such fluid
arrangement go now wordless into
the stream quotidian
waking

white grass crisp
clean air bites
battling entropy

(plump thrush
in the pyracanthus)

opening the fold
reluctant say
warmth a process

begin here now
darkly together
our still song

morning a wonder
accumulates listen expect
don't move
yet

measure the air
obscurely movement
rises in silence

the mind forms
slowly discover
sleeping fumble

wait (preoccupied)
a signal breath
language inadequate

our low bed
assemble the world
ply over ply

synergy's focus
day these moments
various loves

morning I wonder
attend the stillness
runs & pauses
sleeping she holds

a sliver of moon:

orion in the garden

## Ballad: Of Breath & Sleeping

dust             stress             pollens

to begin again: luminous silence
follows your struggle for breath
(an organizing principle) forward
our lives reflect
              focus & rhythm
these are called triggers

the airways contract
              produce
a moment's suspension terror
releasing the expelled attention
distracted anticipate nothing

to nominate proxies: dust   stress
pollens the incessant exposure
to others
            love cannot guard
the delicate lining words
cold air bites

            a mirror
I see you in our children's faces
substantial improvement
the clear air effects
simplicity still your breath
re-centred    I listen to air

this new thing   a music
we cannot predicate
the onset of thunder distant
voices I rise against morning
your breath stilled      sleeping

cold air wind

the cut grass

the flowers

the spring is difficult

remember

wind again listen
weather dominates
our exercise

eyes puffed purple
blotches anger
an ontology

to deal with irritants
directly or sleep
in sympathy

exercise           infection

calm now
our children
sleep

& you
I wait

relief in silence

.

calm
now our children sleep

& you I wait

.

relief
in silence
calm

.

now our children
sleep & you

I wait relief

.

in silence
calm

now
our children

.

sleep
& you
I wait

.

relief
in silence
calm now

.

our children
sleep

& you
I wait

.

relief

.

in silence
   calm now
our children
   sleep

.

& you
I wait
relief
in silence

the onset of thunder

distant the day is organized
(roughly) to meet these needs

space   time   control & avoidance
a tiredness I cannot feel

but feel this love now simple
co-ordinates of breath & sleeping

| | | |
|---|---|---|
| dust | stress | pollens |
| cold | air | wind |
| exercise | | infection |

the onset of thunder

# WHAT IS A MOUNTAIN?

*On Friday May 17, 1975, at about 5:30 in the evening, three car bombs exploded in the centre of Dublin. One was in Upper Parnell St., one in Talbot St, and one in South Leinster Street. At 6:58, a fourth bomb went off in Monaghan town. In all, 33 people were killed. While no organisation claimed responsibility for the bombs, it seems likely that British Army Intelligence were involved. To date, nobody has been arrested in connection with these murders.*

*All art is entirely useless.*

Oscar Wilde


If they ask questions
*skilful poets will know;*
  bright this art you hear of:
  questions the door to knowing.

Gofraidh Fionn O Dálaigh

It is a movement. It rises. Stone floats. It flows. Don't argue.
There it is.

It sits & waits. A small one: see it. Old Bawn. Balrothery.
Templeogue.

Gorse & pine. A map of its contours. Ruin. Wisps of smoke.
Pine again. Road.

Brown-yellow. Yellow. A green. Another. Others.
It is pressure. Petrified.

What is a mountain? Stone flows; folds. A name. It rises.

It divides. It is divided. Rubbed down. Bare. Streaked
limestone. Granite.

Six. Or three. Or none. A mass of extruded matter. A wave.
Irregular. Don't argue.

It is a sentence: syntax, grammar, meaning. It has no meaning.

Clouds gather. Lift. Gather. A frame. Surface irregularities.
Go to it. It will not.

It will not come. It is coming. A process. Fact.

Shape traced. Faintly. Stone delineates. Cleft.

## Tiny Pieces

scattered
this glass
reconstitutes

folds
determine

follow
the lines

come
again

sun
after rain

luminous
leaves

boxroom
window

various greens


a pair of thrushes

first
the world

next
the word

imperfect
charting

close
now

slowly
come

touch
call
remember

simple
pleasures

here
where

all
is

tiny
pieces

## The First Fold

                      now
            city
    sleeping

            floats
    breath

            above
                  green
            still
       mass

the rich interplay between
work & silence
moments remembered
language elucidates

blandly these substances
lost repeating
voice trails
expectations swoosh
inarticulate objects

speculations validate
trees outside
tonal profusion
shades (briefly) fill

leaves radiance
lingers interrogate
process distance

```
    images cluster
         ply
            /
              ply
                  sea
           recedes
pools
        the world
becomes
```

faded intrudes
touch the place
lightly love

possible moment
wisps cling
urban landscape

blackbirds strip
notes accumulate
lyric impulse

scraps of paper
intricate children
catch the odour

quiet garden
name the leaves
gather  tracing

map to colour
latent fog
waves morning

taste moist
(a prism)
sun emerges

speech acts indifferently
factors dominate
light fades long after
sit in the silence

crust dimples
imperceptibly drawing
night slowly
rock flows around

move the weave
out move leaves
turn declining
measure discovery

zone on fire
boredom ignites
questions
conventions

faint trail remains
dispensing blue
a cycle

fine intaglio
song blends over
surface fades

smooth road
coasting canopy
trees beneath
a family

lost now driving
unknown concert
voices melding
night closes

wind between
power & damage
breaking symmetry
associate

places rest
less call snow over
mottled green

ripples
stone makes random
structures & acts
    o call

quietly
numbers simplify
dream of order

rain's consistency

dark against
morning cloud
shifts (verb)

climb & bend
a mountain
restless

rain again

time
return

touch
    lightly
mark

erase
    confine
the line

above
    mass
sleeping

    green
now

    city
      floats

    breath
still

## Aisling: Tits Nesting

press incomprehension space
storage & retrieval
30 years to reach this
whisper long song words
inadequate world
arbitrary symbols
complexity falsified
exclude intractable facts
to make a system
smithereens asking
directions a function
inventing conceptions
not understand life
beyond us beyond these
lines number a language
nature indifferent
nothing we need give
our questions limit us

blue tits flit a whole
feeding imperatives
quince flowers against
the window frames
gratuitous beauty
sit quietly wait
absorption predicates
genetic survival
speed the essence
home here where
life demanding
questions a certain
restlessness locked
inevitable growth
decay wind moves
moving the stillness
provisional sleep
to hold birds' instincts

separate thread wind
entered here we crossed
bridge new love spoken
measure the dance
tree outside indicates
air's movement spring latent
cold sunlight birds' frenzy
building a home retrieve
familiar stability
instinct with meaning
still moving silence
knowledge the only
uncertainty predicates
(fail again) modesty
there are no answers
ready the tree
remaining precise
descriptions may fleck

evasive instance
flit apparently
random effacing
nature protects urgent
refused the given
particoloured sleep
impossible air
dream an ideal writer
failing essence
inessential branches
exemplify
theories of meaning
it's all plámás
rain slants window
does no such thing
imperceptible flows
necessitates time
not order not chaos

idyll is idle is
inescapable power
voices displaced
still silent
speaking invisible
look a word attend
particulars a fair field
stars drift & we recede
shifting vectors
tremble adamant
endlessly out
adorn this emptiness
who sailed who saw
wonders aloud
the world remains
relentless my news
the tits' engagement
unnameable known

not essence but accident
there is no we do not
go there food & shelter
sun warms the quince
peony ivy darts the birds
invisible traffic beyond
words come discretely
gold on grey breeze-blocks
green against green
locked into
dependency baulks
inexplicable name
nesting remember
I do not wish
denial unravels
is not speculate
morning's unclarity
pied against

pinkgrey sky
on a grey hail
what would you say
the writer's intentions
small neglected
child's wonder
fear & uncertainty
quotidian arc
frost on the grass
outside love's permanence
softness hides
scarred granite
intense fragility
her limbs sing
accept nothing
random events
birds' caution
the living landscape

find ambiguity
none intended
imagined relations
sunk in complacency
place each stone
deftly inscribe
integral objects
to empathy time
illusions of permanence
enters this moment
the flowering lattice
engendered weave
fragments a home
constructed the process
wisps encumbered
the rush of signals
turn the form
outward show meaning

night insinuates dark ablatives
remember evading
explosive responses
tearing the air
fractured integrity
these lost these missing
trees felled & the land abused
screaming metal clear illustrations
indiscriminate force
an exercise in power
alone at the edge of things
blue tits construct
outside the mind's
constraints coherence
difficult interlace
scraps attenuated
vision everything
*an apple from wave to wave*

clear now begin again
love of the little things
the world needs nothing
listen to stone
the tits integrate
our artefacts dream
quotidian places
delicate melody
beyond our range
obliterate flesh
nests the rain
turning away
the line resist
song resolves
not entirely
this lonely road
darkness of darkness
they went down

eyes/lips/hands the play
bright memory saw her saw
tight blue against
curves climbing
woman not symbol
not breathable follow
vision imperfect
pattern disintegrates
walking the morning
sun behind movement
palpable swing
bright no explicable
music the day makes
tension between
light & silence
insignificant ball
a 30-year war
distance no object

tits insistence
drives day onwards
measures of quantity
contingency wrought
insidious radiant
wait this lead now
urge an instrument
tender construct
melodic range
progressive guesses
distance accelerates
exploding fragments
day's normalcy
white & whiter
gestures revive
accepting nothing
complex relations
draw herewards

rooting action
rewriting history
expansively sleeping
carry the air
conjunction of tones
melding the notes
find the key
sun the breeze
hearts light
voyage inwards
resisting leaves
inoperable growth
nesting memory
recedes the line
searches tedium
completed the birds
pressure confined
expects no redemption

# The Second Fold

*It is an area. A mass. Perform*

*The great wave of stone. Movement. Fusion.*

*Seskin. Venus. Tibradden.*

```
floats
        still
above

        city
mass

        now
green

        sleeping
breath
```

not sound

not silence

lost in the mountains
        cross
light & air

bite into
stream constructs
an image order
syntax cold

curve suffused
carried forward
morning come

silent voices
enter again
turn not hoping

slow descent
insects block
formal gestures

obey compunction
flicker strategy
unravels daily

swirls of meaning
lost can't:

(this road leads nowhere)

(been there) shift
imperceptible
effort sustains
deplete the growth

slow economy
traces of light
(stone) cloud over

reformulate weave
simplicity falsifies
leaves turn slowly
distant rumble

pressure lines
small bounds here
question slowly

favoured rain
island rising
morning subsumes

transient density
working from notes
patiently laid

walk to school
sodden air
reluctantly come

folding strata
time exposed
home again

smoke low on the slope
in a patch of sunlight
(contingent) a way to work
insistent delay inevitable
now is folded stream flows
matter deleted confirms
nothing delivers light unbearable
sleep
      or watch attention
expanding control a weave
material (stone) on stone

drifting sleep
peel & strip
transverse section

sun & air
passes shift
to sign/significance

faces wait
a panoply
brief intention

dream a tree
suspended here
bole the dance

grow
      (quietly)
more
inscrutable

silicates
sediments

tiny
rain

lost
an island

interface

stone

sleeping
    green
now

    breath
city
    above

      still
    floats
mass

## Immrama

**One**

Go outside. Walk to the bus-stop. Wait. *Do it again tomorrow.* Call this earning a living. Use your time wisely. Join others on the journey. Leave them. Arrive. See wonders on the way. Pellucid dawn. Rain grey. Dew in the garden. Balloons trapped in a bare tree.

**Two**

Long walk on a straight road. Passing traffic. Ribbons of black bin-liner tied to bare trees stream in the sharp wind. Measure the stages: home to garage, garage to roundabout, roundabout to lights, lights to corner, corner to work.

Evening classes.

**Three**

Frail craft in a strong current. An island. Another. This is not fiction. Ride the surface. Wonder. See a new dawn daily. Love unexpected.

**Four**

From then to now. Sailed. Together. Towards uncertainty. Small increments. Remissions. Returns. Distant voices tell. Refrain from telling. There is no.

**Five**

Smoke. A trace of. We went out. The world a complex system of interactions. Walking: crisp air against the skin/breath. Resistance impossible. Arriving to ask the necessary question. Knowledge slips out of focus, not being the world. And then came back again. the story is not in the going.

Snow.

A list of names. Places.

Here it is. Here.

**Six**

Next day same place another. Lit a fire and waited. The great wheel rolls burning down to the sea: collateral damage. Lost one here; the walls turning. Onward.

Sea a constant. Moonlight. Distant voices. Just because we don't understand doesn't mean there's nothing there. Drift aimfully. Home is where.

**Seven**

A bright, fine Friday: I must have been 19. The four of us walked together up South Leinster St., and passed the car about 40 seconds before it exploded.

Picked myself up. Looked back. Saw things I have no wish to remember. People, hundreds, came running. We walked on in silence, but for a repeated, repeating *clack*. Found a piece of bodywork embedded in the heel of my right clog. Pulled it out. Threw it away. Walked on.

Silence.

**Eight**

And then:

Held each other holding each other each held. Other. The same place daily. Food & shelter.

Number these lost ones. The missing. *Do it again tomorrow.* Learn to remember. Faces. Turn for home. Waiting. The car.

**Nine**

Distance cannot. Me memory. Me. Nor time. Darkblue nightsky. Trees against. Walking homeward not knowing.

Where that is.

## THE THIRD FOLD

*images*
  *cluster*
*ply*
  *ply*
*sea*
  *recedes*
*pools*
  *world*
*becomes*

  *latent*
*fog*
  *waves*
*morning*
  *taste*
*moist*
  *a*
*prism*
  *sun*
*emerges*
  *fine*
*intaglio*
  *song*
*blends*
  *over*
*surface*
  *quietly*
*fades*
  *touch*
*lightly*
  *mark*
*erase*
  *confine*
*the*
  *line*

```
green
    breath
now

    mass
city
    above

        still
    floats
sleeping
```

out of chaos
night

out of night
hope

out of hope
the process:

silence:

uncertainty dominates
our lust to order

hesitates
delights in
forms

scars
the memory

words
find

life
endures

flesh
rent

glass
tears

      (clack)

swirls

      (clack)

saw
(tentative )

embedded
fragments
mountain
moves

death
in the streets

light
unyielding

(clack)

*loving & giving*

friday & shattered

in this place
this happened:

death in
the scattered
sunlight

severed
limbs

a silence

metal

idea
into action

time
a device

now
is night

come
quietly

come
to the dark

floats
    sleeping
still

    mass
above
    city

        breath
    green
now

## Love Knots

look she
is here
is not

bird
in the gold
green sings

smiles
&
his brother

smiles
&
his mother

whose
hand
warm
is
laid

who is
not love
a knot

is lost
now not
who is

sweet
this song
is not

meaning
my sons
asleep

listen
to catch
a breath

rain washes grey

light lost behind

or other
words
are lost

*Templeville Road beneath bluepink stratos a colour not either
sky burns intensely beyond low line of houses
the temporal city enfolded in time clouds turn crimson  greyorange
fades
love is sufficient the sky is not ours beyond the low line of language
and the fifth is where you are:*

*relative space a line beyond noise of traffic hills and sky    a
circle
this world exists plain a spread of lives sleep now dream of nothing
ask nothing now this world (delete) frugal means give everything*

*now enter the stone the dark a door open the closed make images radiant
form suggests forget-me-nots    cabbage boats    a water trough
close the open elder & may (a hedgerow) gone to housing rooks nest a
stand
of poplars crisp moon stars a son enthralled mirrored again mind's nature
naked against grey or clearest blue intricate lattice of living twigs*

LOGICAL FALLACIES

this song is not
the world is

this song is not
the world

clear in crisp air hills
road curves banks carmine
grey beyond stratified
light obliquely
starlings & rock
in dream wake integrity
energy discrete flecks on
a small ball turning
outer reaches sweet
insignificance home is

free the word
place is
out there

place the word
here stripped
not there

strip the word
is the place
free there

here & now taste actual
world a word net delivers
illusions knowing
life effaced

dreaming we buy
the things allowed
select signified

nonsense ingredients
economy drives
myth of involvement
nothing seems

if a tree
yes the
question is

air compressed
expanding
earth is

there yes
this air
unfolding is

trees swift stream below
may in april listen
driven to mate
not cause: contingency
marginal difference
accumulates

nearly familiar places seen
daily walking or be
here is new remove

comfort in numbers
do it she said continuity
5000 years

car park trees invisible river hills
misted distant not overtly
out there each clusters discretely
things that are nothing
happening here

moon is here
light clear
in the garden

now is night
come ambiguous
in the garden

moon is come
quickly here
in the garden

make
matter
wave

remember the way
we did these things
are indispensable

breathe sweet air
a single chord
notes blend

the weave of things
particular
love is attention

there is no blue but this
fact of light absorbed
reflected particulate waves
pellucid oh the folds
red soluble stone
motion untypical hinges
the machine allows nothing
stubborn resistance clings

robin
coal tit
sparrow

blackbird
song thrush
chaffinch

crow
green finch
jackdaw

wood pigeon
bullfinch
magpie

who wants hears
no matter        matter
birds in the gutter sing
such sweet lucidity
each discrete note
the fact of it

mimic the thing
be it not here made not
marked reverting ground
life coils around
everything is
not seen or

learning to be
stubborn parts
as energy
to dream of leaving
is not will not be
no other world

wagtail flits a way
in darkness life coils
perpetual change
outliving all
*post hoc ergo*
this does not hold

rain again gleam
these small sounds
we live in
questions the fact
patterns deceive
plash & strive
find place:
first part

PREVIOUSLY UNCOLLECTED WORK

# A Small Book of Birds

robin
hopping
on the wall

blackbird
in the elder
sings

song-thrush
hiding
in the hedge

coal tits
flit
& feed

crows
(grey-hooded)
in the rain

wood pigeon
high
above it all

swallows
(count them)
on the wires

wagtail
skims
across the grass

# Paper Places

**Proem**

for the past 35 years
or so
(you know)
I've been thinking about
how places are written
how poems are found

at first
I thought to educate myself
(you know)
the usual stuff:
poetry
philosophy
linguistics
deep ecology
quantum mechanics
even literary theory

but recently
(you know)
I've tried to keep it simple
& think about the things
that poems & places share

& first I thought
they both exist
(you know)
close the book
& the poem's still there
humming with energy

waiting impatiently
turn your back:
the room's still there
the river's flowing
the rocks erode

& then I thought
they're systems
each part in place
to make the poem
the place
& they are
what they are
(you know)
remove one part:
everything changes

& then I thought
they have
(you know)
location:
the road in
the previous page
the distant mountains
can change the way
you read a place
you see a poem
& so
each system's locked
into a larger whole

& then I thought
if stories
& stories
can be lost

or broken up
or known to just a few
or found in books much later
or known to everyone
or reconstructed
(you know)

& then I thought
that they are made
& Bill talked
(the other day)
about the Alps
& how the snow's
made fresh again
each night
by teams of workers
& the skiers never know
it isn't new

& poems
are made of language
of words and syntax
(& maybe some ideas
or feelings even)
but then
(you know)
the question is
did someone make the mountains?
did someone make the words?

& then I thought
that they evolve:
this city
was once a village
a forest

a desert
the ocean bed
particles spinning
in what we so naively call
the primal soup
& who among us
driving from home to work
to shop to home
would recognise
the westron wind
the small rain
& yet
(you know)
we'd lie with our loves
again

& then I thought
they both have names
& associations
(I said this was simple)
& these two worry me
(you know)
the quick descent
to cliché

& then I thought
one last thought
(maybe a last thought)
they both have uses
(I'm still working on this one)
places have uses
are used
& poems
well
(you know)
I don't know

## Alt Pallars

at this height nothing
matters words repeat
meaningless noise
code broken stone
flows beyond
perception expressing
proteins select these
simple things

## Annacotty

this small world
does not exclude
the greater

house
a spread of houses
a plethora

words flow
here sing
lost now

oh westron wind
& wagtail
hesitates

before
the sound
of mowing

## Bettystown

which brings:
diversity

which brings:
survival

nothing
replicates

days
endless

lapping
sand

## BIRDHILL

a bird
a hill
it's fair

road
curves
under

a wood
slow
through

## Carnsore

dig
a trench
this deep
& long enough

scaffold
& plank
to build
convenience

& they
will come
play here

this power
turns
& turns

## Castleconnell

this river
this constant thrum
these rocks & islets
these birds

> grey heron
> mute swan
> mallard
> dipper
> grey wagtail
> sparrow

a place
grown &
made

these trees
this bend
a cycle
(what happens here)

fields slip
over
defences

park & wall
direct the eye

to cows
& trade

shaped
this flow

## Coonagh Roundabout

such clarity under
dawn not
rose

things etched
good
& beautiful

air drained
morning
is reason

order floats
carved in
water

bare
branches
glow

## GRANGE

this dance
these

stones
placed

come here
expecting

nothing
lines

reason
escapes

## Dover, New Hampshire

something
started here
or didn't
in the woods

a squirrel
sharing meals
outside
heart of

empire breathe
& read
to trail
the singer fall

incipient
storms roll in
a wall
connects us

white it
isn't:
alternate
either

## Lincoln Place

remember
entropy
pieces fly

place
as monument
scarred wall

words
(death comes)
remember them

## Lough Gur

things are
& are
unplanned

we drift
& drift
in time

patterns
of use:
provisional

came here
& lived
one time

## Manor Street

gate
walk
garden

snails
trike
blue

trough
float
stairs

string
cards
school

lodge
street
gate

## OLD KILDIMO

crossroads
pub
car park
abandoned house

road
field
ring of trees

church
(not a church)

school
(not there)

graveyard
(not seen)

## Phoenix Park

listen: not one
but many

come here
walk & play

set patterns
line memory

is motion
actual fall

this place
revolves

time is
& is not

now night
comes

## Rialto

a bridge
& love
came here

to sleep
not quiet
this house

but here
things grew
again

## Shanagolden

it's a real place
it is
we went there

## Shannon

riddle us
this noble name:

old river
particulate
flow

troops
& munitions
ends here

town
from nothing
whose

life
is transit
well

knowledge
sorrow
ends

hazel
she eats
& knows

our lies
their lies
what lies between

## SHERLOCKSTOWN

the smell of the toilet
the mangle shredder
the path the cows used
the horse and donkey
the cans by the gate
the shady orchard
the beehives
the haymaking
the night train passing
the hungry pullets gather round

a place loved
a grudging love

## Tara

these stories
we tell ourselves
these stories

tangle of hazel
golden corn
transient fame

noblest hill
rational language
look now

teeming mound
whence the name
desolate

earthworks
see nothing
leave again

# Two Rivers

## *Mulcair*

## *The names of the water*

Mulcair

Cauteen

Newport

Annagh

Doonane

Mulkeir

Glasharloonaraveela

Bilboa

Cahernahallia

Dead

learning to live here
now effaced
provisionally still
but active
memory
where things have
places
no longer
moving

light &
food suffice
honesty
an ease of
being together
unique each stream
growing itself
call this thing
this thing

words wrap
around themselves
& are not there
beyond
a wall
forget-me-nots
blue &
nothing matters

but life
remains in
small things
house     gate
a wall besides
games extemporised

leaves
    wood
& water
days

placed &
certain because
this sense
made possible
dappled river
arched branches
delight
  flows
through

abstraction
easy evades
location shifts
names indeterminate
play not here
in ordinary
acts &
incidents exceed
the necessary
counterweave

still images show
nascent
air survives
its context
& is
revived
living & sung
(the work
to get the place

in the poem
the poem

in the place)
everywhere spent
actual oak
vivid
with birdsong
rook or
blackbird
packets of
life
this delicate
point
between sentiment

& system
spring is
slow &
how do we live here
& not destroy
the very
place this
tree is
just a tree
birds not
emblems

& we
expropriate
these songs
cannot be sung
simply here
indifferent under
all we make

change imperceptible
scales
home is

not
needs answer
what next
love a field
& fields
structures
weeds
scrub maybe
hazel

wood
a forest
if we were not
this would
revert
rather evolve
this place
this proper scale
seeds blown
insects
birds

the time
that trees make
making trees

Leather-brown oak leaf on the beachwood floor. Pinnate. Dully shining. Shed by the tree across the road some months back; a thing among things, a structure, a name.

The leaf is what it does; a site of interchange. Each one unique despite the single code. Part of a process, a way of making, an adaptation. It decays but is not lost.

Nothing is lost.

Photosynthesis, respiration, transpiration, guttation, veination; the things you name are these. The question of where this is going; back road to somewhere else. A system of delicate tracery enabling. The great, enduring weave of what is. The ten thousand things.

look again:

the river you name
is not
this water flowing

these houses
trees
oak, ash, elm, willow
others

I do not know

& down
to the river

\*

we build
& what we build
has consequence
as if

this time were
everything
a part

(apart) these
words generate
nothing

slip
as water

spaces

between
as they live

in me in
poverty

the will to
learn
accumulate

always
these mountains
also beyond
perception
the earth these
houses lacking

permanence
the river does
nothing

happens
sets of
confluences

packets of self
replication eddy
& dart many
names force
incipient

this system
memory links
not numerous

not light not
after rain after
aglow this
morning

morning
slabs of sound
of wheels engage
electrons flow

& what

they are

## *Time and change at Annacotty*

ford ➔ bridge

mill ➔ bar

creamery ➔ superstore

village ➔ sprawl

fields ➔ roads

river ➔ amenity

to move
& why
& to what end

drifting

slow

*

not why or how
stuff happens
pick

one a feature
or a story
a hero

confuse it

pick carefully fruit
to hold between
an index &

fall: picture complexity
by these hours
as interests accrue

perturbs fine clouds
(how bright time)
are all inured

*

oh it flows
out now
streaming &

nothing pure
remains
beyond this

★

Sun
        Moon
                Mars
                        Mercury
                Jupiter
        Venus
Saturn

★

having begun
already
or before
beginning

come
sit
listen
sleep
now

small
resistance

in the sheet
of things

left
for no
good reason

\*

drift and make
headway
map the shore

or watch

mouth
or bone
are multiple

mouth
not bone
converse

\*

for these words
& these
& this

for being here
now
& now

no one
to thank

\*

wind & rain &
wind & sun &
trees & rain &
leaves & wind
& rain

★

still the silence
still the sound
still hearing
still aloud

still a voice


★

here            here
here            here
here here here  here
here            here
here            here

## *on the bypass*

kestrel hovers
over grass

& drops
as I drive past

## *Liffey*

1

came here
& near
a source

one
of these:

poetry

craft

wisdom

2

lake
bog
willow

the sea
is near

the way
circuitous

slowly
turns
slowly

runs
a trickle

trickles


3

slowly it turns
slowly flows
turns & flows

between fields
between time &
a hedge against

stone & brown
bog swirl past
fire past whose
house whose

sisters three


4

these tiny events that make a life:

sun & rain sound
of children taste sweet
or glimpse hidden
a moment

as these needs
as beauty

calm

quiet

as small things
particulate transform
render tolerable
bring

as these

as it comes down
as it circulates
source to mouth

it enters
it proceeds
it merges

as its name is

as it gives force


5

there were three sisters lived there once:
one to weave, one to show, one to make things grow

in a small quiet place on a small quiet road

bees drift lazily through the orchard

horse grazes in the far field

a rhythm of cattle, of milk

& one went south & one went west and one remained behind


6

small road in the mountains
flat space grass cropped
water flows great stones
cold & smooth
the same river twice

the same child walks

& down down down
& under
feed memory

brown here water is
cold & clear brown bog
cotton gorse above granite
in scud light

granite & shale
goats clamber among


7

to remember one
told stories
at every stop

the work on water
canal        mill
to have entered
the same river twice

weight
on the shoulder

& sun gone now
splendour
memory
same river
same genes
stream


8

as if a river
as if it flows
as if

under grey stone
great arches
canal goes over
this placid water
these plains
this commerce

between stone
water will
be medium
motion between
a principle

to bring down

9

& then came down to the river
in the cold days after the fall


10

would it be so if

what is
the status of memory
of meaning
(a memory)

of questions

to have fallen
to have never seen
as it is seen

to turn back
the system
a part of

oh flow now
to this my city

& as it were
night & warm
humid air

enters
this space

11

the small everyday things shine

a word a gesture
cloud say
or grass a bird
rain in the gutter
light

arc of what happens
& slides between trees
willow & beech limestone
weir light broken flash
cusps of light cut dazzle
ripple between leaf & water
slow refraction bends traffic

a small place
a corner
an opening out
home


12

a map of water moving
down to save to meet
the sea our needs the city

in these times of water
of rising
the tide turns

as these words
as I write them
as they speak

not water but
a certain form

these words
as you read them
as they flow

not water but
its resonance

different & clear
our small deeds
against the tide

# Moon
*i.m. Dee Mills*

## One

beyond the barrier
on the roundabout
above the motorway
as we drive back
to see you

as you fight
for air
for blood
for life oh life

crescent
recumbent
reflected light

in this space
between rain
& rain

dark draws near now
& the moon against it


## Two

the wind the trees the city
road out round & over
the river the fields floods
across this small island a ribbon
lights in motion constant

uneven flow that passes
for life

      cloud always
darkness always night driving
all before sunset hazard
sky filled with stars
moist air exhausted
as it drifts

        the great bowl open &
empty light filled liquid
a space moon pales all

**Three**

three apples in a bowl
the bowl on a table
the table under

under the window
the room is empty
dust on the sill

two apples bruised
they smell of sugar
sugar & must

**Four**

half moon wanes
morning drive
    such

light untold
unsingable

waves numb words
exhausted
        fail
this day there
there is nothing too

absence say
absence that
        there
is this thing
& no answer

moon moves through
& earth moves
        through
& days pass
nothing happens


**Five**

& this
is everything

slender crescent
in air in

space path
recorded

ring arranged
so

to extract
meaning

alignment
& so

to light
imagined

**Six**

& you miss them

the ones gone
the others
who were here
& now are not

sliver of light
reflected

& beauty
there is & is
stillness before
rain a second
time passing things
made & made over

slipping

lost

**Seven**

dark

moon circles
as we circle
repeats

no need

to stop

to get off

to stop


**Eight**

silent moon
quarter moon
half moon
full moon
new moon
crescent moon
gibbous moon
waxing moon
waning moon
blue moon
country moon
wet moon


as if it were
as if

to stop
to get off

**Nine**

the moon is not
indifferent
it is

cells multiply
without purpose

no

without motivation

no

inadequate

try again

**Ten**

trickle over rock
full     full
a pool a stream
spring air filled
cloud    droplets

all before swift
end a question
how to live here now

make patterns
sustain them

crab endures
winter cold
tholes

where all is water
air filled
earth saturate
memory laden

who is besmirched
by this tide
this flow of light


**Eleven**

a certain stillness after rain
night        lie in bed

or

sun between trees by the road
I drive to work     a sound
remembered grey stone wall
by the drive disks of honesty
its seeds river unseen beyond
fields empty night again
not once but often here now
no veil between

such clarity depends
on nothing urns stillness

never felt no other
sense on        light falls
everything glows slow
bathes a single flower

**Twelve**

to be in light
unaware
simply here

not one
not many
over

moon illuminates
reflects

a tale
a story told

there were two
who walked
who passed by

one stayed
perhaps

perhaps

www.ingramcontent.com/pod-product-compliance
Lightning Source LLC
Chambersburg PA
CBHW022000160426
43197CB00007B/201